I HOPE YOU KNOW

Ashley Mescia

Copyright © 2022 Ashley Mescia

'I Hope You Know'

All rights reserved.

ISBN: 978-1-914275-81-4

Perspective Press Global Ltd

DEDICATION

I wrote this for me, a girl who found comfort and healing through her writing. I wrote this for my friends who I've witnessed time and time again have their hearts broken and question if they'll ever be worthy of love. I wrote this for you who needs to be reminded of how special you are. I wrote this for the kindest souls who nearly lost themselves in a world not so kind to them. I wrote this for anyone who will feel less alone through my words. I wrote this for anyone who doesn't feel they are enough on their own. I wrote this for the broken hearts that haven't broken yet but will find this book when they need it the most.

Sometimes the story isn't about what you can't have, it's about what you can become.

Sometimes having a heart of gold is worthless in the eyes of others. They might not see how unique you are, how special you are, or how much you're willing to sacrifice for them - but one day, you will find the right crowd of people who will see all of what you're worth.

Treat your energy like it's your home… that special place where you live and be conscious of who you invite in. Some people will invite themselves just for a place to stay; others will stay because they enjoy the company. Know the difference.

Some people often say no heartbreak will ever be as bad as the first. And for some that may be true, but in most cases, it's not. The first is always going to be one you remember because at the time it's a foreign feeling and something you're trying to navigate for the first time without any familiarity. You're yet to know what it feels like to come out the other side or how to heal from something that causes such pain. Though, this doesn't make any other heartbreak less significant; as you grow and evolve, so does your love for different people. You will cross paths with people who will make you fall so deeply in love that you'll barely remember the last. They will become a distant memory that will no longer trigger the same emotions they once used to. Until it happens again. Your heart breaks a second time. A third time. Each time feeling just as brutally painful because in the moment you are so deeply in love. But look back in hindsight and recognise that every time your heart broke, it also healed. Your heart mends and you become stronger each time. It doesn't mean those people weren't right for you, they just weren't your forever. Each one of those individuals were perfect for you during that time of your life and they all contributed to your growth and learning lessons. In different stages of your life, you will grow and evolve and sift through different partners until one day, you find your forever but until then, don't let all those heartbreaks interfere with your faith.

Be so content in who you are alone that if someone wants to walk out of your life then wave them out the door. Not in a way where you are happy to see them leave, but more so in a way where you are thankful for the time you two shared and the place they held in your life. Acknowledging that your time together has expired and trusting that there are so many more people you are yet to meet who are also going to hold a significant place in your life is powerful. They too may not stay forever – however, every new person that walks in and out of your life is going to bring something valuable with them. I hope you know these feelings of hope should inspire you to remain on the path of self-discovery.

In this day and age, we are surrounded by other people's wins. A girl you knew in school posted that she's getting married, your neighbour just bought a new car, a work colleague just got promoted, and you're sitting here alone right now feeling like you've failed because you think you're not close to accomplishing any of that. Maybe on some days, a win for you is to just make it through to the next and that is totally okay. That's also worth celebrating. It's important to remember that everyone shines in their own unique way; other people's success won't push us further back on our own paths. Other people's success is not the absence of our own. Do not wait to be happy in your own life to be happy for others. Everyone's time will come, including for you. Our wins can be as small or large as we make them. There is no blueprint to survive this crazy world, nor is there a finish line we are racing to. Stay in your lane and don't focus your energy on what chapter other people are on in life - not everyone's book is written the same.

I know how much you're hurting but don't let them turn you cold-hearted - no matter how badly you've been mistreated in the past. For so long, I beat myself up over things I wish I did differently, wishing I didn't do so much for someone who perhaps took it all for granted. I was filled with regret for so long about doing so much for people who probably didn't deserve it… but then I slowly learnt that all those parts of me are not my weaknesses; they are my strengths. It taught me how much love I have in my heart and how much I give to those whom I love. Those are not qualities I should be ashamed of. Then I realised I must not be so hard on myself because if it wasn't for those experiences, I wouldn't have learnt to have boundaries, and I wouldn't have learnt who deserves my love and who doesn't. I'm not going to stop loving just because some people didn't know how to appreciate it. One day someone will, and they'll know how to love all of those parts of me properly. That pure heart filled with love is what makes you so special and I promise one day you'll find someone who will not misuse that. So again, no matter how bruised they left you, do not let them turn you cold.

Change your perspective. I'm a firm believer that rejection is redirection. The day you surrender to what's happening around you and have faith that everything is working in your favour, is the day you will be set free. Maybe you had to lose them so you wouldn't lose yourself. Maybe the exact thing you didn't want is the exact thing that needed to happen for you to evolve. Maybe that job decline was because something better is waiting around the corner. Little did you know, these closed doors are protecting you from paths and places not meant for you.

Save some of you for yourself.

One of the biggest things heartbreak taught me was that no matter how much you love someone, you must not give all of yourself to them - please take that from me as someone who once did. The more my feelings grew for them, the more they consumed me entirely. I never felt this way about someone before and my heart never ached this way for another person. I was so scared of being hurt and left heartbroken that I thought I needed to give them everything I had for them to stay. There's nothing wrong with wanting to give to another person because maybe that's one of your love languages like it is mine, that's how you show your appreciation to another person – as long as you have boundaries. I learnt that when I love, I love hard. Throughout that period of my life, I gave them as much as I could while never expecting anything in return but as time passed, it suffocated me because my whole entire purpose of living became dependent on them. I completely lost myself. I spent months filling up another person's cup to the point where mine was left empty. I was so terrified of being abandoned and left in a million broken pieces that subconsciously, I was already slowly breaking. If there's another thing I learnt, doing so much for someone still won't always be enough to make them stay. What I was fearing the entire relationship is exactly what manifested, and I was left with no choice but to piece together all my broken pieces. It taught me that being heartbroken isn't so scary after all, because even though at the time it felt like my world was crashing down, there were so many beautiful lessons that came out of it that the old version of me didn't know before. It taught me how strong I am and that the only person who can save me is *me*. It taught me that's not what long-lasting love is supposed to be like. It taught me that in the future I will hold on to some of those parts of me for myself, so I don't lose myself entirely again.

I hope you know one day someone will walk into your life and show you why it didn't work out with them. You won't be the one giving your all; you'll find someone who gives just as much as you will. You'll finally meet someone who wants to help you grow in life and will push you to be the best version of yourself.
Your supporter, lover, and best friend all in one.

Ashley Mescia – I Hope You Know

We as humans are wired to always be wanting more than what we have, but you truly will never be satisfied if you think your happiness lies within something you haven't yet got OR something that someone else has that you don't. Because the second you reach that destination that you said you'd finally be "happy" at, you'll already be looking for what you want next. Unless you really learn to find gratitude in everything you have in the *now* and appreciate every little moment before getting there. You can have goals and things that you desire but if you're constantly in a state of *lack*, nothing beyond what you already have will feel like it's enough. Today social media makes it so easy for us to think what we have isn't enough but, we all have so much that's valuable in our lives and there are so many things every day that we can be grateful for.

It's going to be okay. It's okay if you haven't figured it out yet. It's okay if you are scared. It's okay if you need to ask for help. It's okay to let people go. It's okay if you want to change your directory. It's okay if you feel lost. It's okay to admit you made a mistake. You're human, it's going to be okay.

Their inconsistency doesn't determine your worth. Their lack of effort doesn't determine your worth. Them not reciprocating the same energy doesn't determine your worth. You determine your worth. The second you realise that you hold the power in your life, and you get to decide the value of your worth, you will no longer put your energy into things that drain you, or people who don't add value to your life. Because you simply know you're worth more than that. You don't have control over external influences or how people view you, but you do have control over your own standards and what you will tolerate. When you finally realise this, instead of taking it personally, you will recognise that inconsistency as another person's inability to see your worth and respond accordingly by prioritising the people who prioritise you.

It's funny how we outgrow what we once thought we couldn't live without, and then we fall in love with what we didn't even know we wanted. Life keeps leaving us on journeys we would never go on if it were up to us. Don't be afraid, have faith & find the lessons.

Someone's inability to see your worth doesn't make you worthless. How they view you or treat you isn't a reflection of the person you are but instead, it's a reflection of them. One person's "I don't like this about you" will be another person's "I love this about you". So rather than sitting around and questioning if you're good enough for them, start asking yourself if they're good for you.

I know some days you feel sad and lonely and wonder if you're ever going to feel the same amount of love again, but please promise me you won't lower your standards and go back to what hurt you - just to feel that level of comfort again. Because all that love you held for that person didn't come from them, it came from within you. Which means you still have it all within, you just need to redirect it back upon yourself. Give back all that love you use to give them and give it to yourself.

Nothing will ever be taken away from you without the intention of it being replaced with something better.

Love is meant to feel easy. It's not meant to be constant highs and lows with no in-between. It's not meant to be hot one day and cold the next. It's not meant to leave you questioning where you stand in their life, it's not meant to be draining. It's not meant to be sleepless nights and tear-filled pillowcases. It's not meant to bring you confusion. It's not meant to cause you anxiety. At the end of the day if they leave you with any of those thoughts or feelings then you should already have your answer.

If you love them, tell them. Tell them how much they mean to you. Tell them how much you appreciate their company. Tell them how beautiful you think their smile is. Tell them how grateful you are to have them in your life. Tell them you love their laugh. Tell them you're proud of them. Tell them they make you feel happier when they're around. Society nowadays is making us think we are weak to show our emotions but let's change the narrative. Those few words could be the one reason they hold on a little longer.

I lost myself because I was so afraid of losing someone I loved so dearly. From now onwards I'll take my chances on losing someone before I lose myself again.

It's okay to outgrow people who had the chance to grow with you. Don't shrink yourself to fit into someone else's box. Think of your bond as if there is an elastic band between you two. The more you continue to grow while they stay still, the more resistance you create and eventually that elastic band is going snap or you're going to get pulled back. Know when it's time to cut the rope so you can go be the person you have always destined to be.

The right ones will know how special you are, and they won't put themselves in a position to lose you.

Stop being so much of a people pleaser, especially if it's at the expense of your own happiness. If you're spending all your energy filling up other people's cups and pouring from your own, you won't have anything left for yourself.

They pushed you away because they couldn't handle how good you were. They couldn't accept everything you had to offer because they knew they couldn't give you what you deserve, but it's not your job to wait around for them to change. They must want to change, but until then, you need to be strong enough to walk away; love yourself enough to know what you deserve and be secure enough to know you will be okay on your own.

Life is too short for regrets. So, love the people who treat you right and forget about those who don't. Believe everything happens for a reason. If you get a chance, take it! If it changes your life, let it. Nobody said life would be easy, they just promised it would most likely be worth it; So, make it.

That time, a year ago, I thought I was never going to feel how it feels to be happy again. I remember so vividly I was laying on the beach by myself crying and asking the universe to please make the pain go away. The days when the pain was so intolerable, and they weighed so heavy on my mind that I had no room for other thoughts.

Fast forward to now and I feel like the most me I have ever felt. I'm surrounded by amazing people, I'm living in a beautiful place I can call home, I've found the best relationship with myself, I've healed from things I never thought I would, I've learnt so many life lessons that younger me had no idea about. I'm glowing differently than ever before. Making new memories, laughing again, meeting new people, and seeing new cities.

If you're going through a tough time, I hope you know that no matter how grey it looks, there is a light at the end of the tunnel, and you will get there. It won't look like it right now, but time will pass when you can look back and realise how far you've come. Healing or any sort of progress is not linear. 1% improvements every day are hard to notice at the time but when you look back after months you can see how far you've come.

Try not to hold onto false hope or "what ifs" because it's only going to halt your healing process. Understand that you did the best you could with the knowledge you had at the time. Try your best to accept it for what it is and if it wasn't a mutual decision then I know that would make it so much harder, but you deserve someone who wants to love you as much as you were willing to love them. It just means they weren't right for that and one day you'll find someone who will reciprocate all of what you want to give, and it will be worth it.

I hope you know you deserve to be spoiled and loved infinitely. You deserve someone so amazing who will spoil you with not just flowers and materialistic items but someone who will spoil you with the softest most caring words on the days you feel you need it the most, someone who will shower you with compliments even when you haven't asked. Someone who doesn't find it weak to express how much you mean to them.

It's okay to not have it figured out yet. Social media puts so much pressure on us to think that you need to have accomplished something at a particular age or time in your life. It's become a place where we romanticise the hustle and everyone posts their highlight reels and successes, which might make you think you're not doing enough or accomplishing enough at your age. Where you are right now is exactly where you need to be, don't feel discouraged if you think you aren't moving fast enough. Don't be so hard on yourself, everyone's path is completely different and rather than fixating your energy on what other people are doing or achieving, focus that energy on yourself and make yourself a better person each day. Other people's level of success doesn't take away from your own nor should it be used to compare to what we've accomplished.

No matter how much someone you love betrays you or hurts you, you're still going to love them; because at the end of the day, your heart and intentions were pure, therefore you can't just stop loving them so quickly. It's important to acknowledge those parts of you because they don't make you weak, they are your strengths. If you can hold all that space for the wrong person, imagine how much you're going to be able to hold for the right one.

You're always trying to find excuses for the things they did to disappoint you and make reasoning to invalidate the way you're feeling. I know you're always trying to see the good in people and honestly, that's a beautiful trait to have but sometimes you just need to look at things for how they are right in front of you.

If they have the audacity to disrespect you and your boundaries, you're also disrespecting yourself but sticking around and allowing them to think it's okay to treat you that way. Your self-worth is not negotiable.

Taking risks is scary because they require us to go outside of our comfort zone into a world of unfamiliar ground. I hope you realise the answer will always be no unless you ask. That risk could change your life for the better or worse but if you don't at least try, you will never know. You will always be left wondering and thinking about what *could* have been if you had given it a try. So, take that risk, push past those limiting beliefs and pour your entire heart into it. If it doesn't work out, at least you can say you tried and gave it your all. Most of the time beautiful things grow and come from stepping outside of your comfort zone.

One person's lack of effort is not a cry for you to try harder. You shouldn't have to earn your way into someone's life and doing more for someone isn't going to make them appreciate you more. Who you are is enough.

Be okay with knowing that not everyone will be for you, and you won't be for everyone. It doesn't make either of us a bad person and it doesn't make one of us better than the other. It just means we are different, and our differences don't align and there's nothing wrong with that.

Everything happens *for* you - not *to* you. When you begin to look at every major shift in your life from this lens you feel a sense of freedom, knowing that everything happens for a reason and the universe knows what's best for you and your higher good. Sometimes the things we want aren't always right for us. All of those heartbreaks, job declines, and rejections are pushing you closer and closer to what *is* for you. I hope you know whenever you're asking "why is this happening to me" it's because there is a reason.

Please don't ever let another person tell you what you should and shouldn't do to your body. Please do not change yourself for their validation. I had bleached blonde hair my entire teenage and young adult years and I loved it; it became my identity and a part of my personality. I was always so hesitant to dye my hair back to my natural brown, but I never understood why other than the fact I became so attached to the way I looked being blonde. Until over the years, I realised I had so many boys tell me to never dye my hair a different colour because in their words "I suited blonde", "I look better blonde", "I love you with blonde hair". Subconsciously I was so resistant to ever change hair colour because they made me start believing I won't be deemed as "attractive" or as "likeable". Why for so long was I letting male validation decide what I should and shouldn't do to my body. Don't ever let someone make you think you are more attractive based on a certain hair colour, how you dress, or the way your body looks; and if they do, then they aren't your people. I hope you know the right person will see beneath the surface and find you beautiful for so much more than the way you look.

Don't let anyone or anything take your light away from this world. The way you light up when you talk about what you love. The way you beam with excitement for things you're passionate about. Some people don't like to see you happy but that doesn't mean you need to dim yourself to make them feel comfortable. I hope you know that there are people in this world who want to see you shine brighter.

I wish you could see how beautiful you are through the eyes of others. I don't just mean the way you look but also the way you carry yourself. The way you sprinkle your kindness over everyone you meet - no matter how they treat you back. The way you smile even on the days you feel like crying. The way you see the best in them even if they give you many reasons not to. The way you're always trying to fix others while you're still broken. The way you give back to the world after all the storms you've been through. The way you still forgave them after how they mistreated you. The way you put others' needs before your own. The way you still give your heart to people after the number of times it may have been broken. I hope you know that there are so many qualities that make you beautiful.

Change your perspective: they didn't leave you, they lost you. It's not your job to show people your value, but if they can't see it, then back yourself and walk away. Love yourself more than them.

Self-care isn't just face masks, a fresh pedicure, or a new hairstyle; it is having boundaries, saying no to something you don't want to do, it is understanding your worth and not settling for anything less, it's going to therapy, its respectfully cutting off toxic friendships that no longer serve you. It's doing things that make your soul happy.

Givers need to learn their limits because takers don't have any.

If you lose someone who happily walked out of your life, did you really lose anything?

If you feel like you're constantly having to prove yourself, then they're not right for you. If they loved you the right way, you wouldn't be questioning your place in their life.

One day they will look back and wish they treated you differently, but by then it will be too late, and you will have found the one who treats you exactly how you deserve from the beginning.

This past year I've been making a conscious effort to be more aware of the things and people I'm investing my energy into. Asking myself, are they adding value to my life, are they inspiring me to be a better person and how does being in their presence make me feel at the end of the day. Reflecting over the years I feel I've naturally been a big people pleaser, I found myself always disregarding my own needs to put others first and just having absolutely no boundaries for myself. I was always saying yes to things that I didn't even want to do or just giving my time and energy to people who weren't inspiring me to be a better person or making me feel good. Along my self-love and healing journey, it has truly taught me that self-love isn't just about working on loving the outside parts of you but it's also about protecting the parts of you that other people can easily access and being more conscious of who and what you give your energy to. The second I started setting boundaries for myself, I realised how much more I began to attract high vibrational, like-minded, genuine people and anything less than that just fizzled away. I was no longer letting my energy run freely to people or places that were taking it without my consent. I found these handful of people brought amazing energy into my life that don't make me feel drained but if anything, they make me feel inspired, motivated, and happy. After everything, I hope you know what belongs to you is out there. Your soul tribe are out there, don't stop searching.

Good hearts do exist.

Please do not lose hope. I know there are so many times you've wondered if real love still exists, and if it does, you question if you're ever going to experience it. You've witnessed too much heartache and pain that you find it hard to believe anything else exists. You've had no positive experiences to associate love with so now this is all you believe love is.

There are pure hearts out there - you just haven't been exposed to them yet. I hope you know they do exist and when you finally come across one, you will realise *why* you never gave up looking. *They* will be the reason you never settled for less. *They* will rewrite your meaning of love. *They* will show you that real love still exists.

Forgive yourself for all the things you wish you did differently. Forgive yourself for the pain you put yourself through. Forgive yourself for the mistakes you made. I use the word mistakes lightly because, in my eyes, mistakes *mould* us into the *people* we are today. The fact you're wishing you did something differently shows that you would change the way you handle a similar situation now. And to me, that shows growth. If it wasn't for our mistakes, how would we know our rights and wrongs, how would we know for better or worse. We are human and there is not one person who hasn't made a mistake. We have the ability to grow into better people through learning from our past.

Why are we so afraid to let them go? Is it because we don't want to come to terms that we need to rewrite our life without them in it? Is it because we aren't ready to accept that someone else will potentially fill our spot in their life? Is it because we can't bare to think that everything they did with us they will do with someone else? Is it because if we let them go it means they are no longer ours? Is it because they filled a void in us that we don't know how to fill on our own? Is it because we will never get to hug them the same ever again? Is it because if they move on faster than us, that means they never cared? Is it because we can't comprehend how they can possibly love someone else the same way they loved us? Is it because we are afraid we might never find someone like them again? Is it because we wish things ended differently? Is it because we are holding onto a potential 'them' that doesn't exist? Is it because of a false hope that things will get better? Is it because we are afraid that letting them go might be a mistake that can't be undone? Is it because we can't bare to see them treat someone else how we begged to be treated?

Letting go of someone means having to let go of our ego as well. All those reasons we are so afraid to let someone go is because of our ego. Our ego is the root to our sense of self-importance and self-esteem. The harsh truth is that most of the time when we let someone go, we WILL have to rewrite our life without them. They WILL move on and find someone else. They WILL tell another person they love them. It is inevitable, and it is a part of life. But the beauty of it is that so will we. Sometimes you just need to wish them well in the life they have chosen and let them go. Because holding onto something that isn't right for you is also holding you back from finding what is meant for you. As unfair as it may feel sometimes, the faster you accept the reality and undeniable truths of letting someone go, the sooner you will be able to seek what you are really looking for and find who you truly are within.

You keep asking yourself what you did to deserve a pain like this. A pain where your heart feels like it's been ripped out of your chest and your stomach tied in a knot. All you want to do is give love to the world and it repays you with an ache that almost doesn't seem fair. Let me remind you that you don't deserve the pain, you never did; but maybe you *needed* it. You needed it to show you that what you thought you wanted was not what you deserved. Maybe it was a catalyst for you to flourish into the person you have always destined to be. Maybe it was to shine light on all the unhealed parts of you that only you can fix. Maybe it was so your skin could grow thicker and your walls become stronger. Maybe it was to teach you what you thought love was, in fact, wasn't. I hope you know with a heart like yours you never deserved that amount of pain.

One day it will all make sense. I promise. It will make sense why what you once wanted wasn't what you ended up with. The nights you spent crying over them were because there was something better waiting for you. The days you spent questioning your place in this world lead you to people and places you didn't even know belonged to you.
I know some days almost nothing makes sense; you struggle to understand why this is happening to you, but I hope you know one day it will all make sense.

Treat your energy like it's a luxury. Access to you is a privilege and your heart is worth protecting so don't let people walk all over it.

Stop for a moment and feel proud of yourself. You need to give yourself more credit for how far you have come and the things you have achieved. It doesn't matter how small or large they are but don't undervalue yourself. We are all our worst critics, learn to speak to yourself as you would to your best friend, family, or anyone you love. You're changing and growing and evolving. You're not the same person you used to be and for that, you should celebrate how far you've come.

When is it my turn?
You're surrounded by romance and fairytale love stories, constantly asking yourself how one person can meet their soulmate at 17 and I'm in my 20's and have never been in love. How can they have been through 4 different love interests while I haven't even experienced one. As happy as you are to watch everyone around you fall in love, deep down it hurts a little while you wonder if you will have that feeling one day.

I hope you know, no one's life is planned the same, we are all on our own paths and I am a firm believer that you will meet your person when the time is right for you. People meet their soulmates when they are 20, others meet theirs when they are 30. You can't put the expectation on when you're going to meet your person because it's only in the hands of divine timing. So, until then be your own best friend, partner, carer, and lover.

All your flaws and imperfections are what make you, YOU. Isn't it so amazing that not one person in the world is the same as you? We are all so unique and have something different to offer so instead of trying to hide the parts of you that make you stand out the most, embrace them.

Some days just seem a little harder than others. It feels like you're hanging on from a thread with not much left to give. And there's no real reason you feel this way, but you do. Your usual tasks feel like a chore and the littlest things feel way too heavy to handle. On these days be kind to yourself, be compassionate and be patient.

I hope you know that whenever these days show up, better days are around the corner. A bad day does not mean it's going to be a bad life and ebbs and flows are normal. Your feelings are valid and it's okay if today you simply don't feel like showing up for the world. While this day will pass, I'm sure it won't be the last, but these small moments help you appreciate the better days in the future and from your past.

Ashley Mescia – I Hope You Know

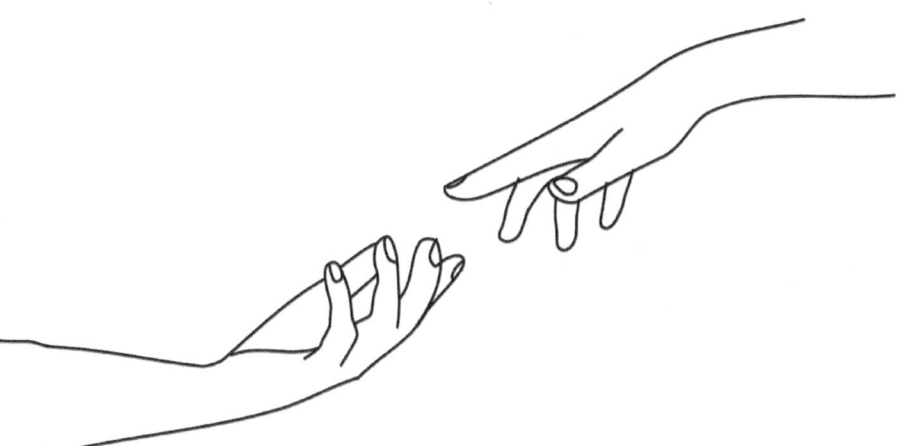

I hope you find the strength within yourself to forgive the people who treated you poorly. The ones who took advantage of the most vulnerable parts of you. The ones whose intentions weren't as pure as yours. Most importantly I hope you find the strength to forgive yourself, for allowing them to treat you that way. I don't mean to forgive them in a way where you are tolerating their behaviour, but I hope you can find that peace within yourself to move forward and take back your energy from anyone that no longer deserves it.

Even the most beautiful love can hurt. The sort of love where it is so real and raw that it takes over your entire body. You feel so much love towards them that the thought of losing them hurts. Loving with your whole heart means having to be vulnerable and let another person in which is so intimidating, especially since doing that last time left you broken.

Meeting them was not just a coincidence or a waste of time. Once upon a time, they were exactly what you wanted, but as we grow, there are things we want to change; it doesn't make your time with them any less valuable. Everyone we cross paths with exchange some sort of value in our life. I'm sure there were numerous beautiful lessons, memories and conversations that grew from your time together.

It's interesting just how in-depth our minds and our thoughts affect our happiness. Every emotion we feel falls back onto what thoughts are going through our head and it's almost scary how powerful that is.
I hope you know your thoughts aren't always reality.

I hope you know you deserve the purest sort of love. A love where it's not too exhausting to send good morning and goodnight texts every single day of the year. A love where a future with you does not bring them fear. A love where they want to listen to all the good and bad from your day. A love where no ounce of distance will get in the way. A love where to them all your flaws and imperfections are what makes you beautiful. A love where they aren't afraid to show how weak you make them feel. The sort of love where any disagreement won't make them doubt you, it only makes them want to grow stronger with you.

From all those times we've been hurt, maybe we've hurt others too. Sometimes we are the ones on the other side breaking people's hearts, hurting their feelings or making big mistakes. As much as you don't mean to, you do. It's a part of life and sometimes it's truly out of our control. You can't stop the wrong ones from thinking you're the right one. Maybe you must teach them lessons and be their catalyst for growth. It doesn't make you a villain, but the harsh truth is we all get hurt and we all do the hurting.

You're only ever making yourself available to what you're choosing to put up with. How do you expect to find someone who's willing to give you the world if you're still settling for the ones who only want you when it's convenient for them? How will you meet the one who wants to wake up next to you if you're still entertaining the ones who only message you after 10pm? Before you ask yourself why you're always attracting the wrong ones, ask yourself if you're letting the wrong ones in.

Do things that make your inner child happy. The older I get the more I realise our inner child never goes away. Most of the unhealed parts of us as an adult end up being what our inner child longed for. The smallest things that make me nostalgic now make me the happiest. I think the older we get the child in us still needs nurturing. So, every once in a while, go to the cinemas the same as you did when you were 5, play board games with your friends, read a book, go to theme parks, watch your favourite childhood movie, and lastly put your phone down and be present in the real world. I think when we are young, we are so desperate to grow up, but life moves too fast to wish it away too quickly.

As much as it hurt me, thank you. Thank you for showing me what I don't want, thank you for showing me what I *do* want. Thank you for showing me how much I can love, thank you for showing me how I should be loved. Thank you for all the lessons I learned and thank you for showing me my unhealed wounds as much as they burned. I hope you know, I am thankful.

I hope the next time you cry, it is tears of joy. I hope you get that job offer you've been waiting for. I hope you get to see your family that you miss. I hope *that* first date was so successful you've already planned the next. I hope you get accepted into your dream university. I hope you reach that goal you've been working towards. I hope you go on that dream holiday that you so much deserve. I really hope something so wonderful happens it brings you tears of joy.

One day you will be able to look back and realise how far you have come. The moment you realise certain situations that would have triggered you a year ago no longer do, is a euphoric feeling that I cannot explain. That's when you recognise how much growth you have made and how strong you were for pushing through those low points. When I was hurting, I was convinced I will never feel okay again, I was in denial when people told me "One day you will look back and it will be a distant memory that no longer causes you pain", I thought that was impossible - I won't ever be able to heal from someone that I loved so much; but I did.
I did it. And so can you.

Someone once asked me- "are you afraid you will never meet someone up to your standards".
I replied, "not at all".
I know those men exist, and even if I were to never meet him, I'll happily stay single for the rest of my life over lowering my standards to settle just for the sake of it.
I could easily settle for someone who barely gives the bare minimum, but if I was to do that then I'm shutting myself off from attracting the person I truly desire, which is someone who's willing to give me the world and more.
When I know how much value I can bring into a relationship and as a partner, I need someone who will reciprocate that. Don't ever feel like you're asking for too much because you will never be too much for the right person.
The stronger you stand with your beliefs and values, you're only ever going to attract people who align with them.

I truly believe what you put out into the universe, it will give the same back to you. Everyone has bad days and that's okay but if you're waking up every day with a bad attitude and outlook then I highly doubt you will be served the best day of your life. Personally, I've noticed the less I look for negatives and I focus on the positives, the more I attract that energy throughout the rest of the day. Being genuinely happy and complimenting my friends makes me feel warm. When I do small acts of kindness to help others throughout the day it makes me feel grateful. All of these small gestures increase your vibration out in the world and in return, the universe will align you with anything on that same wavelength.

If you can't control the situation, you can at least control the way you react to it.

Never feel guilty for doing what's best for you.
You don't owe anyone anything nor do they owe you.

It's okay to let them go. It doesn't mean it no longer hurts or you no longer love them, it just means you're accepting that it's time to leave that chapter in the past and move forward with your life.

I hope you live your life on your own terms. Imagine when you're 80 years old watching a highlight reel of your life and realise how many things you didn't do because of other people's judgement. Imagine realising how many opportunities you missed out on because you feared it wouldn't work out. Imagine realising you didn't follow your dream because it was too far outside your comfort zone. Imagine realising you didn't express yourself a certain way because it was not fitting for society's standards. Imagine realising you made all your decisions based off other people's opinions. You don't want to look back after all those years and wish you spent your precious time differently. Be the main character of your life because if you don't, then someone else will.

I hope old fashion love never dies.
I'm a hopeless romantic and when we meet,
I hope you are too so we can romanticise our lives together.
I'll lay awake till 3 am talking about anything and everything as deep as the universe.
Let's run away on the weekends to unknown destinations and come home with a novel of stories to tell.
I'll wake up in the morning to the smell of coffee and pancakes while you come home in the night to the smell of pasta and wine.
We can park at a lookout and fall asleep under the stars while wrapped up in each other's bodies.
Instead of text messages, we write love letters and keep them to read once we grow old.
Let's slow dance in the kitchen to music and laugh until we cry.
I hope even if old-fashioned love does die, it won't with us.

You'll know you found someone worth keeping when you help each other become better versions of yourselves. Not because you will feel like you need to be but because they will make you *want* to be. It should feel easy around them and no matter how little time you've known each other, it will feel like a lifetime. You will both put your egos aside and anytime a problem arises you will fight it as a team not against one another. You both will add value into each other's lives rather than being an imbalance of give and take.

Actions will always speak louder than words. This goes for any situation - in a relationship, friendship, job, or family. Nothing will ever show someone's true intentions more than their actions. Anyone can easily convince you how amazing they are, how much they care about you and how much they would do for you – even with a few words – that is not hard at all. Anyone can do that. But if their actions are not matching up with their words, if they are not showing you how much they care, if they are not reciprocating the same level of effort you are, that is the version of them you need to believe. To physically uphold "this" version of yourself that you are not for a long period of time is impossible. It requires effort and consistency which are the two things they will lack if their intentions aren't sincere. This is how people love-bomb in the initial stages of relationships. They convince you at the start through actions and words how amazing of a person they are, but after a while, if they can't uphold that version of themselves anymore, it is their actions that will start to fall. So, if you're wondering why this person is constantly convincing you how amazing they are but at the same time always leaving you disappointed, you're most likely holding onto this version of them they are not.

Isn't it a scary thought to think that someone who once had such significance in your life is now a stranger with distant memories. The first person you would call is now someone whose *contact* no longer exists in your phone. The only person you thought about every day and night is now a person you only have fleeting thoughts about every few months. The only person whose life you knew inside and out, you now have no idea what their life looks like. The one person I never wanted to imagine my life without, I am in fact living without.

Can I just remind you, please don't be scared by that. I hope you know they will not be the last person who will have a significant place in your life, and they won't be the last person you share cherishable memories with. As we evolve through different stages of life it is natural for people to come and go. Don't resist letting someone go just because of the history you have together. As you evolve new people will come into your life who will suit all those different versions of you that you are still yet to become. When I first experienced really losing someone, I will admit, it was scary, it was a painful adjustment, and it was hard to accept letting that person go meant letting go of all the history as well. But years down the track I now look back at that period fondly without pain, knowing that person was important to me during that time of my life but the person I am now is completely different to the old me and we wouldn't align the same way we used to. In past relationships, the thought of losing someone caused me so much fear but now it makes me excited to meet all the people I haven't yet met.

A good one.
Is someone who always speaks highly of you. Is someone who accepts you for all your flaws and imperfections. Is someone who never judges you or makes you feel small. Is someone who will have your back even when you're not around. Is someone who checks in on you to make sure you're doing okay. Is someone who supports you with every decision you make but also will be honest with you if something is out of line. Is someone who celebrates your wins like their own. Is someone who doesn't feel intimidated by your success but rather feels inspired. Is someone who will silently listen to you. Is someone who respects you and your boundaries. Is someone who prioritises you.
Hold onto them, and don't let them go.

Your ego is your own sense of self-worth and self-importance, and subconsciously we do things daily to fuel our ego because it makes us feel worthy. However, if you are searching for happiness from other people's validation, materialistic items, external factors, or anything that is only fuelling your ego, you will forever be searching to fill an empty void. Anything that is ego-driven will give you instant gratification, a quick burst of high that might feel like happiness but once that feeling deflates, you're left at square one searching for the next person or object that will give you more of that "happiness". Chase things that light your soul on fire, things that truly bring you happiness deep within things that add real value to your life.

Why in this generation do they find it so hard to appreciate what they have? They're exposed to so many options daily that if they settle too soon, there's fear of missing out on something "better". When most of the time what they think is "better" is something superficial.

Please do not let anyone save you for later. You deserve someone who wants you and you only. Someone who does not question if the grass might be greener somewhere else, but rather works hard to harvest the ground you walk on together. Someone who does not doubt whether better might be out there because to them, they have everything they need. You are more than enough and with a heart like yours, if they can't appreciate that now, then they don't deserve to later.

I know all you want right now is to be loved, to feel loved and to have someone to love; but you don't need to wait for someone else to come along to do that. The only person who can love you without question or doubt is yourself. Stop waiting to put that responsibility in the hands of someone else who might possibly leave you disappointed. Stop waiting for someone else to love you to feel loved. Don't let someone else hold that much of your power. I hope you know you have the capability to love yourself without needing someone else to prove you're worthy of love.

I thought you were everything I wanted until I realised it wasn't *you* I was in love with. It was a potential version of you that I created. Maybe if I believed it enough or waited long enough it would come true. Instead, I was given false promises, unpredictable behaviour, and a love unreciprocated. I thought one day you will be who I want you to be, and everything would be exactly like I was hoping. However, that wasn't the case, so I no longer will chase or hold onto something that doesn't exist. Actually, it does exist, just not in you.

Who said you need to have your whole life figured out by a certain age or in a certain order? I don't think anyone ever has their entire life completely figured out. Even if you think you do, there are possibilities it won't always pan out the exact way you're expecting. Life happens to throw unexpected events at us that aren't even on our horizon. Look at the pandemic for example, that changed so many people's lives whether it'd been losing loved ones, jobs, homes, or health, and there was nothing anyone could do to prepare for the impact the pandemic had on our society. I hope you know it's okay to not have all aspects of your life figured out, it's okay if you want to change career paths in 10 years time because you realise your passions have changed. It's okay if parting ways from a long-term relationship means having to start dating from scratch again. It's okay if some days you feel like life is one step forward and two steps back. Sometimes it's better to not always be so in control and just surrender to the unknown and embrace whatever stage of life you are in right now.

Ashley Mescia – I Hope You Know

I hope you're happy. I really mean it. I hope you know that's all I ever wanted for you. Whether it was with me or not I hope happiness found you, because you deserve it.

Whatever belongs to you will simply never pass you by.
Living with this mentally will set you free from the fear of rejection or anything not going according to your plan. Unfortunately, what we want isn't always what we get, and things won't work out in our favour, but it's always for a reason; the universe has a different plan for us. The person I like doesn't like me back - that's fine, they don't belong to me then. They are not my person and the right one will come along. I didn't make it into my dream college - that's okay, it's not the right place for me, something better must be planned for my higher good. I didn't get accepted into a property - no worries, it wasn't meant for me. The right one will come along. You will never miss out on something if it wasn't yours to begin with.
Being able to look at roadblocks and path changes through this lens is liberating and it's important to remember where every door closes another one opens. Even when I don't know the answers, knowing that there is a plan for me and that what belongs to me will eventually find me, is enough to ease my pain.

I think the most beautiful thing you can do is kill people with kindness. We often are encouraged to treat people how they treat us, but I don't think that's what you should do. I think there's nothing more beautiful than carrying yourself with grace and pure love no matter how poorly you've been treated. Throwing shade will never make you shine brighter, and you shouldn't ever feel you need to prove a point to someone by lowering your dignity. The way someone treats you is a reflection of themselves so whatever you respond with in return you are only projecting attributes of yourself too. No matter how fragile they make you feel, the fact they will never be able to take away your kindness to me shows more strength than anything. Be the one person that makes people still believe there is kindness in the world.

You're still standing tall after how many times you've been knocked to the ground. You wear your heart on your sleeve regardless of how many times it's been ripped apart. You always manage to find the sun within all the clouds. You light up the room with your smile every time you walk in. I hope you know that your strength will take you to more places than you could have ever imagined.

I hope you know there are so many qualities that make you attractive yet have nothing to do with the way you look.

Your kindness, your generosity, your respect, your love, your intelligence, your work ethic, your strength, your positivity. Attractiveness should never solely be about having a small waist; it should never be about having a certain hair colour or skin colour. It should never be about how popular you are. Of course, we can be physically attracted to people but it's shallow to judge someone by only what's on the surface. If someone ever makes you feel valued only by the way you look, please let them go. There are so many people in the world who will love and admire you for much more below the surface.

I think the older I get the more I value quality over quantity. I'd much rather have two real true friends than a large circle where I'm spreading myself too thin. I'd much rather have deep conversations about the meaning of life than small talk. I'd much rather emotional intimacy than meaningless sex. I'd much rather early nights in than late nights out.

Why did it sting a little inside when I found out you moved on after I thought I completely healed from you?
I hope you know that's normal. I don't think you ever fully heal from losing someone, I think you learn to live without them, and time heals most parts. I think healing and moving on also comes in stages. Each stage brings up different emotions and healing is about sifting through those emotions as they come up. Most of the emotions are at the beginning when you're grieving, but it's okay if a year down the track something still triggers you. It's okay if checking in on them after a while brings back old emotions. It's okay if seeing them move on two years later does as well. They are all different stages, and it becomes a different kind of pain. Rather than an ache as if your heart is on fire and continues burning for months, it's more of a dull ache, it doesn't last long, and it just passes by. You feel it and then let it go. You can be certain that they are no longer what you want but still have a soft spot for them. At the end of the day, you are grieving someone you love and seeing what was once yours, become someone else's.

Every girl you find you look for her.
The truth is you will never find her.
She was one of a kind.

Don't let someone damage you so much to the point where every person that walks into your life next makes you question their intention. Don't let someone break you so bad that you're too scared to trust again. Don't let someone hurt you so deeply that you sabotage every good heart that comes past because it almost seems too good to be true. Don't let someone make you believe you couldn't possibly be worthy enough to experience a healthy love. Don't block yourself from experiencing real true love because of one person's poor example. I hope you know there are people who will want to give you their heart and it's not fair to them or yourself if you think everyone's interpretation of love will be the same.

What will it take for us to truly love ourselves?

When I gained weight I wanted my smaller body back, but when I was 10kg lighter I still didn't think I was small enough. "I'll be happy once my skin clears up", but once my acne cleared up, I then wanted to alter other features on my face. I started lifting weights to grow my muscle, but once I started, I didn't want to get thick thighs. I kept picking myself apart and finding things I needed to change because of my false perception of "perfect". I think it's totally acceptable to enhance our features if it means making ourselves more confident; I'd be lying if I said I haven't had anything done. But it doesn't always mean it will make us happier. It doesn't mean we will be completely satisfied. Comparing yourself to other people will forever be the thief of self-love. It's simply inaccurate and misleading to compare yourself to others when we are all so unique. We all have different bone structures, body types, heights, genes, everything. If we are constantly convinced we will be happy with ourselves once we look a particular way it will be a never-ending cycle of searching for self-love. We will never truly be happy with ourselves if we don't just accept and love who we already are first. I hope you know cellulite is normal, so is acne, and stretch marks, and rolls when we sit down are too. Dark circles, hair on our body, scars, marks, we all have them. I think that's what makes us perfectly imperfect because perfect is not real. At the end of the day, there is no true meaning of perfect. It's a definition made up by society and that social construct is not facts. I have my fair share of days crying about my insecurities, and days where loving myself feels extra hard. I hope you know that's okay. Loving yourself doesn't happen overnight, you can't just wake up one day and say, "I love myself" and it fixes everything. It's a journey, and you still will have days where you have felt better but you will also have days where you have felt worse. It's all about slowly learning to love and accept all the things that make you, YOU and be unapologetic about it. On the days you find yourself a little more critical, those are the days you need to be the kindest to yourself. Sit in front of the mirror and say all the things you love about yourself, even if it's only 1 thing. Start there and then slowly build on it until you can say 5 things, 10 things, and more.

- I love my eyes because the colour reminds me of the ocean
- I love my skin because it protects me
- I love how strong I am because it makes me feel empowered.

I know I've said it before, but our bodies are here to do so much more than look pretty. They are our home, and for that, we should not tear them apart we should protect and love them.

Don't be afraid to be on your own. I think that's when you learn the most about yourself. No one else's opinion or judgement can get in your way. You do not need to compromise for another person. You get to be selfish. It's just you, your thoughts, and your feelings. You vs the world. You get to decide all the things you love and all the things you don't. You get to experiment with your interests and find different things that ignite passion within you. You can casually date, meet new people, see new cities, and try new hobbies. I hope you know just because you're alone it doesn't mean you need to be lonely.

That was my fault. For being too convenient for you. For giving more than I should have because I thought it would bring me closer to you. For thinking that I was not enough for you. For not speaking up about the things I didn't agree with. For all the signs that I should have listened to yet chose to ignore. For allowing myself to be treated as an option. For letting you believe I will always be there no matter how I am treated. For not having boundaries. I've learnt, and those are mistakes I will not make again.

I think we often expect happiness to be a life without uncertainty, anxiety, or pain. Where every aspect of our life is being fulfilled and it's free of worry. Where every area of our life is thriving, and you have not shed a tear in a while. But you can not wait for your life to look like that to be happy. You can not wait for your life to be exciting and beautiful, instead, you must find the beauty in the chaos. You can not wait for happiness to come to you because it can only come within you. Rather than seeking happiness from things happening in your life, it's a byproduct of the life you live. Your life can be messy while still feeling happy. It doesn't need to be a huge milestone that makes you feel happy, it can be as small as having your morning coffee, watching the sunset, or seeing a friend.

And just like that, listening to our favourite song no longer makes me cry. I don't think of you if the same car you had drives past. Going to the same places we used to go doesn't trigger every single nerve in my body. When I see photos of us, I don't feel anything. You're no longer the first thing I think about when I wake up nor the last thing on my mind before bed.

I hope you know all those days you spent with tears rolling down your face wondering if you would make it to the other side, you just answered that question. You did it.

Please do not give up. Your future self will thank you.

I used to stress myself out religiously if things weren't unfolding the way I had planned and if I wasn't attracting the things I was trying to manifest. Constantly running myself through the ground. Questioning what was wrong with me, doubting my ability to achieve what I wanted. However, every single time I didn't think it was going to work out, it did. It always worked out. Even if it wasn't the way I hoped, it always worked out in a way where I was able to reflect and realize it was right for me and it always worked out at a time I was ready. I promise you the hard work will eventually manifest, and you will be able to enjoy the fruits of your labour but until then you must understand giving up will not get you there. Consistency, determination, and commitment will. You never know that moment when you're so close to giving up could end up being the breakthrough moment that leads you closer to your goal. And if you were to give up there is that chance of losing everything you tirelessly worked for. It's so easy to see other people's wins and think how did they get it so easy? It may look like it happened overnight but most of the time we do not see the sacrifices they took. We can not see the sleepless nights they spent. We can not see what they truly went through to get there. From now on I release all resistance for things to happen how and when I want them because I truly know it will work out in divine timing and for my higher good.

My mum always warned me about people like you. Your despicable behaviour hidden by desirable charm. People like you target people like me. You can almost sense the purest sort of energies because we are easier to manipulate, you take advantage of the softness in our hearts because you know we will give so freely.

I call people like that energy vampires. They get their energy source from you and in return, you feel exhausted and drained. They will take and take with no intention to give in return. They will come in and out of your life on their terms, cause a tornado and then you're left with no choice but to clean up the mess. I used to think I could fix them, maybe I could change their mind. Maybe I could heal all their wounds and be the reason all their problems go away. Until I learnt that is not my responsibility. You are not *my* problem to fix. You can not fix someone who does not want to be fixed. More importantly, you cannot help someone who does not see an issue in their actions.

Stop comparing yourself to *her*. You might think he's happier with her, she's prettier than you, she's more successful than you, he loves her more than you, whatever it may be, please stop comparing yourself. She might be all those things, but she is not you. No other person can replace you or the moments you shared with him. Yes, it might be different now when he loves someone else but that doesn't mean he didn't love you. It doesn't mean the memories you made together didn't mean anything and most importantly it doesn't mean that you are less worthy.

There is always going to be someone in the room more successful, richer, prettier, fitter than you but you need to remember that doesn't take away anything from you and what you bring to the table.

I hope you're so comfortable with me that not a day goes by where you feel you can't be yourself. I hope you trust me with all your secrets. I promise no matter where we end up, I will still never tell anyone. I hope you feel so secure with me you're not afraid to show me all your scars. I promise I will accept you for all of who you are and not question a single part. I hope you can trust me; I will not judge you for who you are now or who you were in the past. I hope you know I will always listen to what you have to say, without getting in the way.

She knows who she is, who she's not and who she's never willing to be again.

Before you go, I want you to take everything I wrote in this book with you every day moving forward. I hope my words were able to resonate with you and simply make you feel a little less alone. I originally wrote this book for my younger self who needed these reminders. I wrote as a console to my emotions and never had the intention to share it with the world. Until I realised how many people could find comfort in my words too. If you're ever feeling lost, unlovable, confused, broken, hurting, or simply need reminders, read this book as many times as you need. I hope you know you are loved, you are worthy, you are special, you are unique, and this world wouldn't be the same without you.

Copyright © 2022 Ashley Mescia

'I Hope You Know'

All rights reserved.

ISBN: 978-1-914275-81-4

Perspective Press Global Ltd

About The Author

Ashley Mescia is a 22-year-old girl from Queensland Australia.

She found a huge passion for writing throughout her healing journey. She realized how much it allowed her to express her emotions and with all that wisdom she hopes that others can find healing and comfort through her words.

This is Ashley's first published collection, and this book was inspired by writing everything she wished she could tell her younger self. Now it's a book she can pass down to others and hope it will help them too.

About The Publisher

Perspective Press Global is an independent publishing firm representing predominantly authors under the age of 20. Each summer we open our submissions for those above 20!

At Perspective Press Global, our mission is to inspire young aspiring authors that there is no such thing as being 'too young;' your voices deserve to be heard.

The firm was founded by Eleni Sophia as she struggled to find representation when she was a 13-year-old writer. We now have published young talent from around the globe – including, the UK, Albania, Australia, Ireland, and Kosovo.

If you're interested in joining our team, please visit our submissions page at perspectivepressglobal.com and come say hello over on Instagram @PerspectivePressGlobal

www.ingramcontent.com/pod-product-compliance
Lightning Source LLC
Chambersburg PA
CBHW030305100526
44590CB00012B/531